Unclaimed Baggage

DRE PIERRE

Copyright © 2023 The Moving Pen

All rights reserved.

ISBN: 979-8-9865734-5-8

Unclaimed Baggage

DEDICATION

This is dedicated to Dad (Rest in Peace). You will never be forgotten. To Mom always Love you and love your support. To my daughters continue to be your natural self. To my stepsons stop playing and make your money. To my close cousins, I see ya. To my brothers, I got nothing but love for you. Lol

CONTENTS

	Acknowledgments	i
1	Man Poetry (CP1)	15
2	The Start	16
3	Not Us	18
4	Muted Thoughts	20
5	Overdue	21
6	World Tour	23
7	Ambulatory	24
8	Desolate Deducing	25
9	Following Love	26
10	Man	27
11	Time to Reflect	29
12	Men (CP2)	31
13	Black Coffee	33

Unclaimed Baggage

CONTENTS

14	The Dark Side of Love	34
15	The Assembly	35
16	No Control	37
17	Accident	39
18	The Talk	40
19	Mumble	41
20	Lost Hope	42
21	The Checklist	43
22	When Love Hits	44
23	Twin Flames	45
24	Unclaimed Baggage (CP3)	47
25	Unclaimed Baggage	49
26	Everybody But Me	50

Unclaimed Baggage

CONTENTS

27	Poetic Thoughts	52
29	Seasonal Changes	53
30	The Sound of My Voice	54
31	Redwood Trees	55
32	Summary	56
33	Talks & Hugs	57
34	Unfamiliar	58
35	The Winter rose	60
36	The Wrong Words	61
37	Hidden Words	62
38	Priceless	63
39	Vibration	64
40	Reflection	66

Unclaimed Baggage

ACKNOWLEDGMENTS

The words mumble from my mouth, and I scream:
The sins of a man are reborn in the birth of his daughter and she carries the DNA of a lion,
So be careful if you think she's the prey because
Her roar is inner and Her bite is mental.

Much Love to Destiny and Brooke!

Unclaimed Baggage

Chapter One

MAN POETRY

THE START

Everyman brings a little something with him
when his ligature with a loved one is broken.
That mysterious kiss he gives you is followed by
the notion
that passion has scarred his temperament.
He's no longer that knight running through
darkness to save the princess.
This man has become something different,
and each bag he holds has a story to unfold.

Nameless but never faceless, the memories run
deep
because within a man's heart, there is a child
holding his fears.

As he tries to lay the foundation of a cemented
life, he knows
true love will find him someday buried amongst
his baggage
and that lucky soul will unleash the King beneath
the rubble—
to rise and lead like a man with pure devotion
that will burn this earth,
so he can give you the world…

There are an array of things I learned in life, and one of them is Love. The heart knows what it wants, and there's nothing you can do to guide it away.

NOT US

It's an illusion to seek and think we can become one
when there are boundaries with ideas,
and you failed to become aware of your rumination.
You merely tongue-tied my mind with your vision and concepts.
The perspective of life is Love, so live and move with no regrets.
We are just pawns in a game, and we want the same thing.
But maybe our wants aren't connected
to our dreams…

I can love you and never hold your hand because the definition of love is just that: a description. If your zeal isn't worthy, then we are left as prosaic friends.

MUTED THOUGHTS

I could have told you "I do" a thousand times,
and it would have felt like weights smashing your heart
because you never heard the tones of my vocals,
just the language I used.

You see darkness as a lit hallway,
while my mind finds the light too blinding to stare at.
And you haven't heard anything I said
because your volume is muted when a man speaks with the truth.

My vision isn't through your eyes,
and you refuse to try,
so we end up chasing the dream of couples in love,
where you are wanting me, and I am wanting peace—
and neither one of us hold volume in our hearts.

OVERDUE

Cement is cold in the early morning sun
because it's covered in a dew moist from desire.
I have yet to move any muscles for your anima
and in turn, you call me the one
and try to attach your goals to my mood.

This leaves me to chuckle at the thought
that you are trying to be persuasive,
but you just haven't understood
that man can't be claimed by tribal rituals.

If my hand isn't extended,
then you are not to be offered my energy
because life in itself
has an expiration date,
and we are overdue
on our journey.

There's no greater love for a man than the love for his daughter. This leaves me in my current position of rethinking my role. I'm somehow being claimed like lost luggage waiting to be found...

WORLD TOUR

My destiny isn't defined by my travels.
I speak with an open tongue
and sometimes, as the earth moves,
I shift the other way
like a turtle in its shell
hiding from any breeze in the wind that might
feel strange.

Nothing in life strolls like a thought left on paper,
but my numb feet stay grounded as I look
outward from my hull.
I'm neither emotionless nor heartless—
more like speechless with my sentiment in a deep
pool of water.

AMBULATORY

Life journeys are intertwined with massive adjustments.
We tend to seek that tranquilizing sound,
but know that, with energy, there is no ending—
There can only be transition.

Your dreams are infinite
like love-muttered reflections,
so keep that shimmer and know that light
will always be an amalgamated part of your soul…

DESOLATE DEDUCING

The broken angles of my wings
have grounded my soul from its eternal flight.
I have become as empty
as land that bears no green
and is coated in hard lava rocks.
My purpose must unfold,
or I will be swallowed by
my lonely interpretation of love.

FOLLOWING LOVE

Within my heart
stones and pebbles are consistently being tossed.
My last breath submerges under emotional
flames,
outgrowing the hurricane-force thoughts
pushed on by fragile outsiders
that spew over their own conscious love,
while I stager through the thorns
of an empty rose bush.

Seeking illusions within fabric walls,
I tussle with the idea that my fiber
might be flagrant to a soulful touch.
And somehow, the stench of verbal scars
still soaks my veins beyond the spring-filled lust.
But I remain optimistic like summertime
deliberation
that I will find that red rose blooming
within winter's field of wheat,
and we will swirl like the leaves of autumn
to a tune of old jazz
played with moonshine
as the country breeze
embraces our affection.

MAN

The agitated mind of a man
is lost within the words he mutters
when he says:
"I'm alright,"
knowing the demons in his mind
have infiltrated his conscience
and his goodwill is held up by a toothpick
underneath a boulder
overlooking a cliff and facing the morning
sunrise.

There's a majestic cogitation that I would stumble upon my art and realize the painting I seek was never beyond my measure but more in front of my mirror.

TIME TO REFLECT

We never take a minute
to flush out toxic energy
and allow life to burden our souls
with nothing but beloved propositions
of what we should appreciate:
the laughter of life,
the songs of affection,
a memory that made you smile,
a loved one you are proud to know…

I take my first sip,
and I can hear the words unfold
like the flowers breached by the sun.
My language is poetic,
and I'm overlooking the landscape of life.
Being beyond negative vibes,
I see love amongst dirty sinners.
I connect with vibrant energy
that flows positively like a steady stream.
This is where I become caffeinated by my thoughts
and elect to design a portrait of poetry
with a piece of my heart.

Unclaimed Baggage

MEN: THE RATIONALIZATION OF INTROSPECTION

CHAPTER 2

There's a thought that men can handle it all. The notion of the brave souls battling evil and coming out ahead is all but a fantasy of fiction. The reality is we all need a little reinsurance that we matter—somehow or someway, we matter to at least one person in this life.

BLACK COFFEE

I can feel the vine of my soul drip like black coffee,
and there's nothing to dilute the transparent tone of my bewildered thoughts.
So I step softly through moist cement,
hoping I don't harden the idea of tainted sins
because my thirst danced alone
while my burdens buried my advance,
and now I am sun-dried from the inside out.

THE DARK SIDE OF LOVE

Somewhere between the "I love you"
and "call me when you get there",
there's a misconceived perception
of what piety is supposed to be…

I cannot breathe in tomorrow sins,
nor walk away from the casting of my shadows.
I stand within the breeze
of a man's cold heart
because I know nothing but the words
that have been regurgitated for centuries.

The apple has been partially torn,
and I am just a child with monogamous potential
that knows time—
And I know there's nothing left
on the outer shell,
so I stand with no label for man
to dissect my sanction
and leave me wonderless in cogitation
that love can be achieved when
my heart has burnt the souls
I love.

THE ASSEMBLY

I am foreign to the region,
so I find myself lurking through my twilight
sleep,
for the cellars of dreams have been buried
beyond the darkest night.

If I breathe in life,
I seem to spew out death
to the ears of my solo hunters
who deem me the prey their mind seeks
when I'm only the frame of my inner self
where love used to blossom
to the tune of old R&B soul.

But I'm decayed by the broken heart that I suffer
from,
which leads me on an assembly line
of fiction over facts,
for I can be bold with my words and still,
the solo hunters can't hear my screams—
She believes the assembly line can be fixed
by changing the product.

*I cannot convince a person of predetermined thoughts,
so I'll utter silence over speech to protect the ears of the innocent,
for when you have a battle cry of war,
the madness won't let the conscience think.*

NO CONTROL

I have no control over any rationalization
that might complicate the aura we built
through our intangible feelings.
I try to enclose all emotions
until a final result concludes us as the outcome,
but water can never be held back
when pressure is above heated levels,
my heart seems to be engraved with your initials,
and this cup of our emotions is overflowing to a point
where I may be ready to say I do
before any ink can finalize what is…

*The next chapter is self-insured
and co-authored by my passion
that was lost in a dark space.
I'm seeking my conviction
and I ask for no remorse,
for I am the maker and
illustrator
to my final destination...*

ACCIDENT

I'm floating over sentimental waves
because I'm a man
first and foremost.
So if the tender idea that I care
is too perspicuous from this poet,
you must engage with my intellect
so you can receive the weaved threads of love,
even though my energy can be closed off
if the construction on the road
is due to a toxic accident.

THE TALK

I open my book and stare at the blank page
with nothing but understanding.
I have spoken and you haven't heard
anything but the beating of your heart.
My language has deceived your aura
to believe you are the solo star,
and I am nothing but a mere smudge
intertwined within your fibers
alone
until you have been challenged to see.

The dialogue I have canvassed on these walls
with my art
speaks in the volume
that you have yet to comprehend
because you don't want to hear
what the painter has painted.

MUMBLE

I distance myself from the concrete sidewalk
made by man.
I'm strolling the earth confined by the wilderness
and recognizing that science is simple.

Love is a complicated formula,
for no matter what the truth is,
the ears only comprehend
the sound of rhythmic tones
with various instruments.

We are not on the same accord:
You hear the drums of the beat
while I hear the melody of the piano,
leaving us off-key.

LOST HOPE

The vision I'm too impaired to actually see
has become my delusion that was created on the
day we met.
I wandered off until I hit a dead end
and still remained past my chapter
where my story was on page 49.
It was the simplicity of the love that gathered in
my heart.
Now I'm a lonely straggler seeking a place to
comfort my misery.
Another door closed, and my heart continues to
shrink,
for I only have so many hearts to give
before my well becomes as empty as a man with
no hope.

THE CHECKLIST

Does she make you smile?
Is she understanding?
Is she open-minded
and nonjudgmental?
Is she your peace?
Can you tell her anything?
Can you trust her?
Can you grow with her?

*That's my checklist.
What's yours?*

WHEN LOVE HITS

What I've learn is that you can't control who you love.
You can pretend what you're feeling isn't real,
but in the end, your heart will not lie.
And if you are entangled outside of your web,
you will feel the uncomfortable grip of sin—
That guilty hold will let you know where you truly belong.

And no matter how much you may not want
to hurt anybody along your path,
happiness isn't for you to squander—
Either you seek it out
or lose yourself to what could be.

The choice of your future is clear,
but it remains *your* choice.

TWIN FLAMES

You're the center of my life
when our energies gather like light in dark night.
I know what the mirror of love holds
when I'm submerged in your eyes.
We are connected through centuries:
old lost souls that found a way to unite.
From your skin tone to your witty mind
and smile of diamond gleam,
you understand me because you studied me.
There's genuine care in your heart.
We shall grow old and ride for life
because I know you're my reflection
I acquired from the dark.

Unclaimed Baggage

UNCLAIMED BAGGAGE

CHAPTER 3

I can't hold your heart if my hands aren't ready.

UNCLAIMED BAGGAGE

I sit upon the carousel
waiting to be claimed.
A black bag among so many,
I have no tag
so I can't be named.
I stroll on the metal sidewalks
hoping just maybe, I will be seen,
but I stroll a second time
without anybody really noticing me.

I'm filled with life and adventures.
Within my bag, I have my dreams.
I've been to countless places near and far
and I'm still unclaimed on this metal swing.
I know that when the carousel stops,
there will be nowhere for me to go.
I will be placed in the lost and found,
where Unclaimed Baggage holds empty souls.

EVERYBODY BUT ME

My soul has been stolen
and I've been given a cavernous shell,
for I have been burdened with a grind
that weighs heavy like bags of sins filled with death.

My path moves along jagged edges
layered with knives, guns, and broken drug dreams—
It's a journey a child shouldn't have to hold;
I've seen eradication and necrosis and became comatose.

There's nothing unwatchable when seeing a tortured human,
so my human side overshadows the dark tableau.
This is way too much for a child
That never had time to blink

From the time my first words became poetic, I've displayed a heavy sense of trust that penetrated my shield.

POETIC THOUGHTS

I'm not open to the idea that we have to change
in order to find the beating connection to our
hearts.
That vibe or link we seek should be the
extension,
not the transition.
So if we follow the tune of our harmonic
thoughts,
we should vibrate to a solution,
moving our souls to a destination
where we are at peace
with whom we have chosen—
And that will be the moment
when we say:
Forever is too short
for our love.

SEASONAL CHANGES

I salvaged my meals
like vultures on a roadside carcass.
There was no divergence to my disposition—
Nothing was in my dialect
but stolen altruism until we gazed
at each other with glazed eyes.
And at that significant point in my life,
I knew:
The weather will no longer affect my mood.

THE SOUND OF MY VOICE

There's a moment in everyone's life
when words may thump like rocks on boulders
falling from the sky,
but all we hear is the chirping of birds in the
wind
at that precise time.
So, we need to pause our daily routine
and realize life is more than options—
It's passion and purpose
and filled with lessons.
What would you have learned
if you allowed the noise to be your focus?

REDWOOD TREES

Standing amongst the elements,
I'm fortified by nature's ways of love.
You are like the wind in the mountains.
A greater height will gravitate our bond,
and I'm rooted within your walls
like a fixture built in for a reason.
We are sections that are selected
on an aura of peace, unity, and knowledge
that biodegradable paper can't slice
like a knife to a redwood tree.

SUMMARY

You choose who you choose.
The elevation of amity
goes beyond verbal affairs.
It's the foundation
that outlines the cause.
The effort is the building of memories
that is a result of our ligature.
We speak in fluent tones
of melodic vibes
that we nurtured as life,
and we are living it as the prototype.

TALKS & HUGS

My mood moves with frequent philosophy
and my thoughts are in tune with my slumber.
I know no boundaries when I'm in hunter mode
because first blood has drawn me into your sight.
But my vision is distorted as I manifest my goals,
and this is where I realize that
my life has become an endless passion of lust
as if I turned down the wrong road
because I wanted a solid kiss
with nothing but talks and hugs.

UNFAMILIAR

My boundaries are my priorities,
and I'm centered on being safe.
So if my elastic ideas are being pulled back,
it's because energy matches energy,
and you have become
unfamiliar.

Life is the barren of emotional thoughts,

and I am the center of its play.

THE WINTER ROSE

I heard you whisper those words
that lay heavy upon my soul:
"This isn't for me."
And I felt the Arctic breeze
hover over my heart
like a blanket snatched in the early morn.
My mind drifted underneath the withered rose petals
that fell like snowflakes in December.
I knew the twin flames had burned
beyond recognition,
but to this day, I'm still holding the match
that sparked our love.

THE WRONG WORDS

I'm shattered by my soft innuendos,
leaving me desolate in the open dark.
There's neither a remedy nor a resolution
that can mend the fabric of time,
but we remain loyal with words over the physical
because our hearts didn't get to touch
like our minds were able to love.

HIDDEN WORDS

So our nuance is more like coded language,
we speak with a laugh and giggle,
and I'm holding air as if it's occupied,
knowing its imaginary ideas
are like cartoon characters—
Board games, kids games, fun times to now wondering
what time we have left in the days to spare
under tones and lost souls
and the knowledge to know
where we have been,
but nothing is written
because words are always hidden in between verbs
and adjectives and nouns without sound—
And if there was a chance to look eye to eye
without one word being said,
you know as I know
the flames that we would burn
would be eternal
like verses in the Bible…

PRICELESS

I watch you like a Mona Lisa painting,
priceless,
our bodies blended like a caramel glaze.
We went way beyond our persuasion
and created an organic phenomenon,
flowing like the water of a woodland creek.
I taste more than the fragrance,
I taste you.
I was confused between
erratic behavior and sensual touch,
but I know being with you is like being at my
domicile.

VIBRATION

There was a moment within our conversation
when I felt the vibration of our bodies change—
sort of like a seed planted for growth.

Our verbal meditation is like vines stretching
alongside a brick wall:
We lectured our minds, hoping to dissect every
deep thought.
I am more than intrigued by your melanin-toned
beauty.
You have wrapped your hands around my mind
and drowned me with your sarcastic wit.

I can feel your vibration
and notice there is a simple mood that has
recently changed.
I reach out my hand and wait to see
if you will extend your hand the same way.

A man can encounter a multitude of different women in his life, but there's always one that will motivate, entice, and create that burning fire of love. And that's when time becomes your enemy.

REFLECTION

If I caress the paper, you will accuse me of harassment,
but I can't help but to feel my way through its fibers
and let it gently touch the pen that's going to spill ink
between its margins—
A splatter best left alone
as I raise my knowledge and stand firm in my belief
that I am unclaimed for a reason.

There is no cheat code for my combination;
The source of my aura will know what to write,
and I will then collide in loving harmony
with my eluded twin flame,
for we both recognize the mirror
that stands before our eyes.

As we murmur "I see you",
there's a fire within ignited.
Our lives have scorched this earth
once before,

so I can't bear witness to
a false representation of love
if my heart isn't built
in your foundation.

I HAVE BEEN FOUND!

Unclaimed Baggage

BONUS POEM

DESTABILIZE

There has been a destabilization of our
connection.
We are cycling on different levels,
and our aura flares in distorted colors of a
hypnotic blue.
I'm distant but not lost.
My vitality is a simple location.
There's peace within my mind, body, and soul.
I can duplicate any written paragraphs
with ideas defined with truth.

And know that everything I said
wasn't dissected with logic;
it overrun with love.
Emotion will never let you see
anything within a forest of life.

ABOUT THE AUTHOR

My poetry is my soul. I was born in Brooklyn, New York, and raised in Queens New York City. This is where the sounds of a busy city whispered melodic tunes to the fingerprints of my heart. I'm proud to be born and raised in a city that can easily manifest the most creative ideas. This is where my poetry came to life. I started writing in elementary school. Poetry gave me a way to express myself and my journey began with my first feeling of love. I write with a passion in my poetry, short stories, and songs. Everything I do is with the emotions from my soul.

Also, check out…

"Pocket Love Poetry"

Drepierrebooks.com

www.ingramcontent.com/pod-product-compliance
Lightning Source LLC
Chambersburg PA
CBHW070631050426
42450CB00011B/3159